The Heart Guide

S.G. Thornton

This book is dedicated to my love

Clay Heart

And our three children

Kaleidoscope

Fire

&

Wave

For All Our Blessings

Thank You God

Best Wishes for 2015 S.G. Thornton 1/8/2015

Copyright © 2014 S.G. Thornton
ISBN : 1505315824
ISBN-13 : 978-1505315820

CONTENTS

Illustrations: Mason Bussey Edited: Melody Bussey

Introduction

A couple of years ago I started questioning how people love each other. I didn't understand why or how someone could love a person more than the person could love him or her. I would see people giving all their love without receiving love in return. This was devastating to both people when the hearts were a total mismatch.

One day the answer came to me. People love on different levels. Not all hearts are compatible. Not all people require the love of others to make them happy.

Now that I had the answer I needed a way to explain it to others. I woke up one morning opened the blinds and I remember saying, "Thank You, God, for such a beautiful day". Bam! The Heart Guide was born. Hearts started coming into my mind as fast as I could think of them. Each heart was associated with someone I knew or had knowledge of. As I thought of a person that I knew I could see their heart and each heart was unique.

I remember running down the stairs to share my thoughts with my family. I wasn't sure how they would react, but I knew I had to take the chance.

They loved it. They immediately started writing down everything I was saying and drawing images of what the hearts would look like.

Over the next 24 hours, 13 Hearts had been created. I had an overwhelming sense of urgency to find someone to help me capture the images and the words to describe each heart. It was like God was saying, "I've given you what you asked for. Now do something with it".

I remember picking up the phone and calling my favorite Ghost Writer. Actually, she was the only Ghost Writer I knew and I was confident that she could help me bring the hearts to life.

The pages that follow contain the amazing gift God has given me,
13 Hearts. I hope you enjoy them and have as much fun as my family and
friends have had deciding:

Which Heart Am I?

1

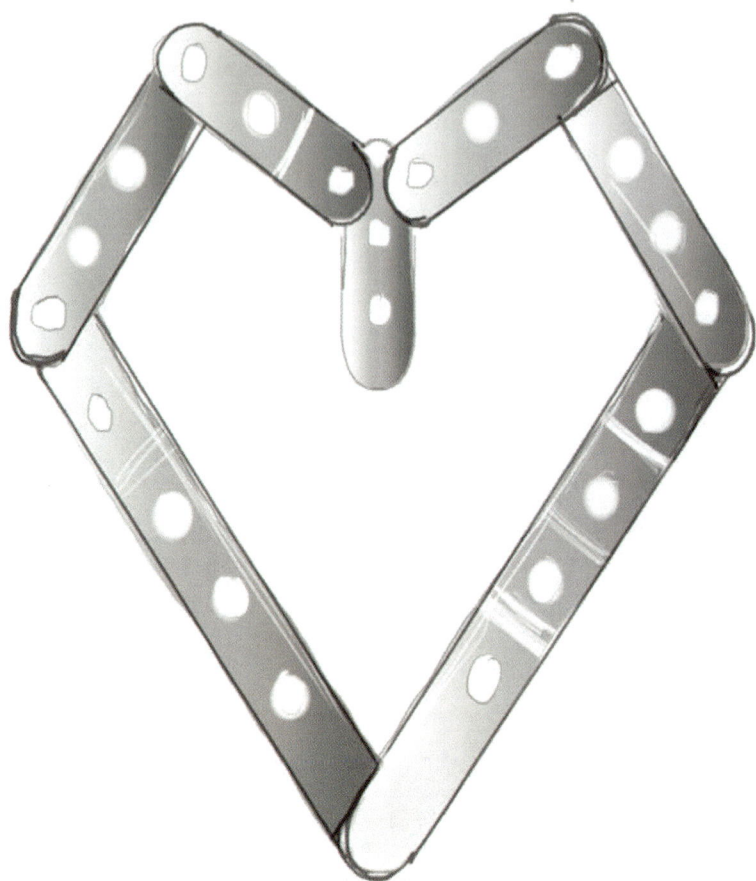

The Builder Heart

The Builder Heart

Intelligent, reliable, and discerning, the Builder Heart has the amazing capacity to quickly size up a situation and begin to formulate a plan. Their greatest strength is the ability to build, not only their own lives again, and again, but also to help build and rebuild the lives of others.

How we love…..

Builder Hearts love to have a good plan. Gifted with a quick and nimble mind, they are quickly analytical, sometimes charging to the rescue with their latest plan and solution. Builder Hearts experience great success in their relationships when they are able to allow themselves to remain balanced between intellect and emotion. Builder Hearts are at their best when they are encouraging others, suggesting plans of action, and supporting creative endeavors. They can be leaders, but are just as happy sitting back and watching others succeed.

How we learn….

Builder Hearts, like Erector Sets, come with many and varied components, allowing them many 'tools' when it comes to communicating and working with others. Older, more mature Builder Hearts know just how much pressure, what type of pulley, motor, or fastener is needed to improve a situation. Their solutions may often seem unconventional, but trust is important to the Builder Heart. The Builder Heart's intuition and hunches are almost always right.

Builder Hearts are extremely organized, and every moment of life is planned and executed precisely.

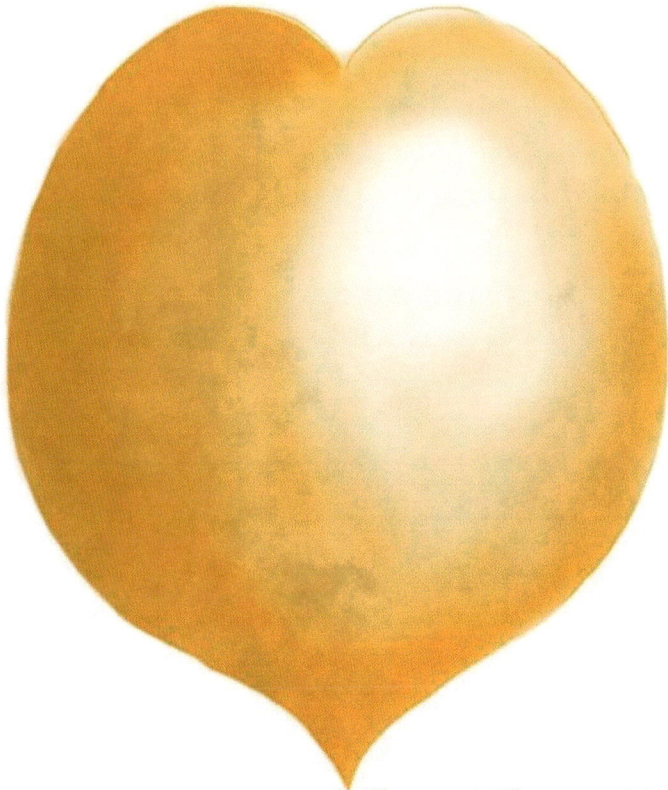

The Clay Heart

The Clay Heart

Adaptable, helpful, and innovative, Clay Hearts are able to fit in anywhere they find themselves. They can be molded, shaped and reshaped over and over. This incredibly versatile heart has as its greatest strength the ability to be what others need them to be without losing their own identity. Clay hearts love to mold and shape new ideas and inventions. Clay hearts are very creative, and they long to teach others what they have designed or discovered. Clay Hearts love to be appreciated, and have the great ability to reinvent themselves at will.

How we love…..

The Clay Heart is a lover and a giver. Both adults & children love the Clay Heart.

Clay Hearts can often go over-the-top when they fall for someone, investing all of their time and energy into them. Mature Clay Hearts realize this about themselves and are careful to support, nurture and care for others, even those they deeply love, while preserving their deep original nature. Clay develops over many years, and is often hidden underground until some great need brings it to the surface. This is true for The Clay Heart when they finally meet their great love.

How we learn….

Clay Hearts love to work in groups and shine when working on collaborative projects. Clay Hearts are ready to jump in and help out at a moment's notice. They are often the backbone of any great organization. Many Clay Hearts are entrepreneurs and small business owners. They are committed to learning one new thing every year. Clay Hearts will have multiple degrees, certifications, and professional credentials. The constant learning creates constant reshaping, which leads to dynamic results.

Clay Hearts love to mold and shape new ideas.

The Porcelain Heart

The Porcelain Heart

How we live….

Charismatic, optimistic, and highly spiritual, those possessing Porcelain Hearts have much to be proud of. Created from extreme adversity this heart emerges from often harsh beginnings to shine with a luminosity that draws others to it, often effortlessly. Most often these hearts find themselves drawn to jobs where their inner and outer beauty has a chance to shine, where they can share their stories, and encourage others to persevere. Porcelain is produced at high temperatures, beginning with a crushing process, and the product that emerges is highly prized because of its translucent properties.

How we love…..

Having experienced the 'refining' process, Porcelain Hearts understand and empathize with others, and often make great counselors and therapists. True Porcelain may crack or chip, but it does not splinter like Fine China. This is because there is a necessary purification process that takes Porcelain one step further than regular China. Like porcelain, the Porcelain Heart has gone through, and will continue to experience, purification processes throughout their lives; a letting go of that which no longer serves.

How we learn….

Porcelain Hearts, because of their deep capacity to be aware of the feelings of others, often expose themselves to more stress than they should, resulting in the fine crack lines and chips. However, with a little polishing and smoothing away, repairs are possible. Porcelain Hearts should be careful and know how much is too much, and when asking for help is the smartest thing to do for everyone involved.

Porcelain Hearts understand and empathize with others.

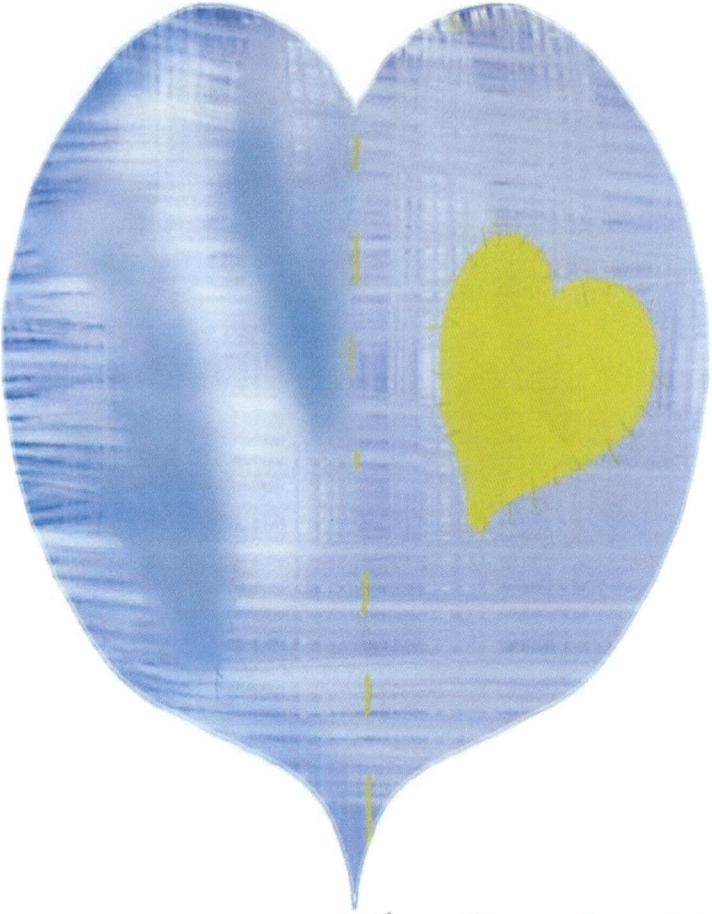

The Denim Heart

The Denim Heart

How we live….

Resilient, strong-willed, and protective, Denim Hearts are not afraid of hard work. Equally at home outdoors or out on the town with friends, this heart loves to be moving, working, serving, and doing. Often these hearts are very aware of their humble beginnings and strive to prove themselves at every opportunity.

How we love…..

Denim Hearts will take calculated risks if they believe that it will be for the greater good of everyone around them. True Denim is created when a combination of natural and synthetic fibers are woven together, creating a stronger, and more durable material. So, too, are Denim Hearts created. Life's fibers combine with a strong inner spirit that may be ripped, torn, faded by the sun, and soiled….but a quick patch and it bounces back ready for action, again.

How we learn….

Denim Hearts don't rip or tear easily, and are easy to get along with. They are often charismatic leaders, and have a great sense of humor. They have the ability to cut to the chase and quickly ascertain what needs to be done.

They don't tend to be fussy people, but have definite opinions, which they have no problem sharing. Denim Hearts when young can be quite stiff at first, but will soften with age, creating a lasting and true friend.

Denim Hearts become more beautiful and treasured over time.

The Wood Heart

The Wood Heart

How we live….

Steady, true, and nurturing, the Wood Heart offers the world the reassurance that life is not all bad. The Wood Heart is as versatile as it implies, its characteristics allow it to be anything from supportive furniture, housing, works of art, and even providing the deep resonance prized by the makers of musical instruments. So, too is the person whose heart resembles wood.

Part of the Wood Heart's strength is that it not only survives, but thrives in all types of weather, through all types of obstacles, adapting and overcoming, and often becoming something quite beautiful as a result. They may be burned, nailed, carved, and sanded, but they never stop being beautiful and continuing to move forward.

How we love…..

Wood Hearts tend to love and trust slowly, and if you get too close too fast you can end up with splinters. Once committed they are devoted for life. They expect the same depth from their mate as they expect from themselves, which can often lead to disappointment. But, never fear, the Wood Heart will put up with a great deal before turning away. The Wood Heart might have old wounds, like nails, that have never healed, but are capable of overcoming the damage and loving again. The nails are reminders of their survival and how far they've come.

How we learn….

Wood Heart personalities often make great teachers, medical practitioners, spiritual leaders, and are phenomenal when working in people-oriented service to others. They are some of the kindest people you will meet, but are also unwavering when it comes to taking a stand for those who may not be able to advocate for themselves. Wood Hearts have a deep-rooted sense of justice and are tireless when working for a cause. They can move people with their words and are captivating speakers.

Wood Hearts are in it for the long haul.

11

The Aluminum Heart

The Aluminum Heart

How we live….

Persistent, courageous, hopeful, the Aluminum Heart believes in the goodness of others, even extending themselves to assist in 'lost causes' when everyone else has walked away. Adaptable and forgiving the Aluminum Heart can be dinged, dented, and scraped, but in the end is able to spring back into shape to take on another task. Aluminum Hearts wear their love on their sleeve and are always ready to help out.

How we love…..

Aluminum Hearts are often given to self-sacrifice to the point that they take on too many causes at once, which can leave them battered and crumpled, especially in matters of the heart. However, if given enough space and time, the Aluminum Heart is one of the most resilient hearts there is. They never lose hope. Embracing their quiet strength, Aluminum Hearts never corrode, never fail, and are lightweight. They do not ever seek to put a strain on their relationships, cherishing them for what they are, not what they may become.

How we learn….

Aluminum Hearts are the supporters, the behind the scenes kind of hearts that make life possible for those who would blindly charge full steam ahead into things. They learn by doing, and are very hands-on and are happier in the field than behind a desk. Aluminum Hearts start from the ground up giving them enormous credibility in all their endeavors. People quickly realize they can rely on the Aluminum Heart and never be let down.

> Dinged, Dented, Bent, and Burled, the Aluminum Heart never loses hope in themselves and in the potential of others.

The Tree Heart

The Tree Heart

How we live....

Multifaceted, talented, and deeply spiritual, the Tree Heart loves on many levels and in many ways. The Tree Heart has deeply rooted beliefs that may be bent, but will not be broken or uprooted. All attempts by others to do so are an effort in futility. Tree Hearts are patient, aware that seasons come and go, and have a very far-reaching, long run approach to each endeavor.

How we love.....

Those who have a Tree Heart are very aware of their own talents and abilities but don't take advantage to hold that over others. Instead, they often seem 'older than their years' in their observation of human nature. They are equally able to love each person they meet right where they are at the time. The young to the old seem drawn to this type of person, and simply 'feel' better when they are around them.

Tree Hearts are only upset when they offer true advice and it is ignored. Their observations are generally correct, their intuition keen, and they do not offer advice lightly. They will remain loyal for life, once committed.

How we learn....

Because of their ability to love and work with people on different levels, the Tree Heart works well with large groups of people as well as one-on-one situations. They learn best when they are left to their own devices; to explore, question, and contemplate the situation at hand. Patience is rewarded because the Tree Heart is seldom wrong in their hunches.

Tree Hearts remain loyal for life, once committed.

The Wave Heart

The Wave Heart

How we live….

Wave Hearts engulf life. Determined, responsive, and creative, Wave Hearts can often assume a larger-than-life persona. Like its characteristic element, water, it can also have a calming and healing effect on those around them. Many people simply 'feel good' after spending time with the Wave Heart. The Wave Heart is able to nurture and surround others to provide encouragement just when it's needed.

How we love…..

Wave Hearts come crashing in to engulf love and to protect. Wave Hearts change temperature slowly, and as such don't often lose their tempers. When they do, it is likely to be done and over quickly. Wave Hearts can slowly erode away relationships that no longer serve a purpose. They are naturally optimistic people, and their perfect partner would be someone who could challenge them intellectually.

How we learn….

Wave Hearts engulf learning, will devour books and possess an amazing recall. Because of their ability to change states (liquid, solid, or gas) Wave Hearts don't tire easily. They have boundless energy, and are often the people who are gentle but effective leaders, never giving up until the goal is accomplished. Wave Hearts are constantly seeking information, gaining knowledge, and sharing that knowledge with others. Wave Hearts are skilled debaters, communicators, and writers.

The Wave Heart plunges into life, love, and learning.

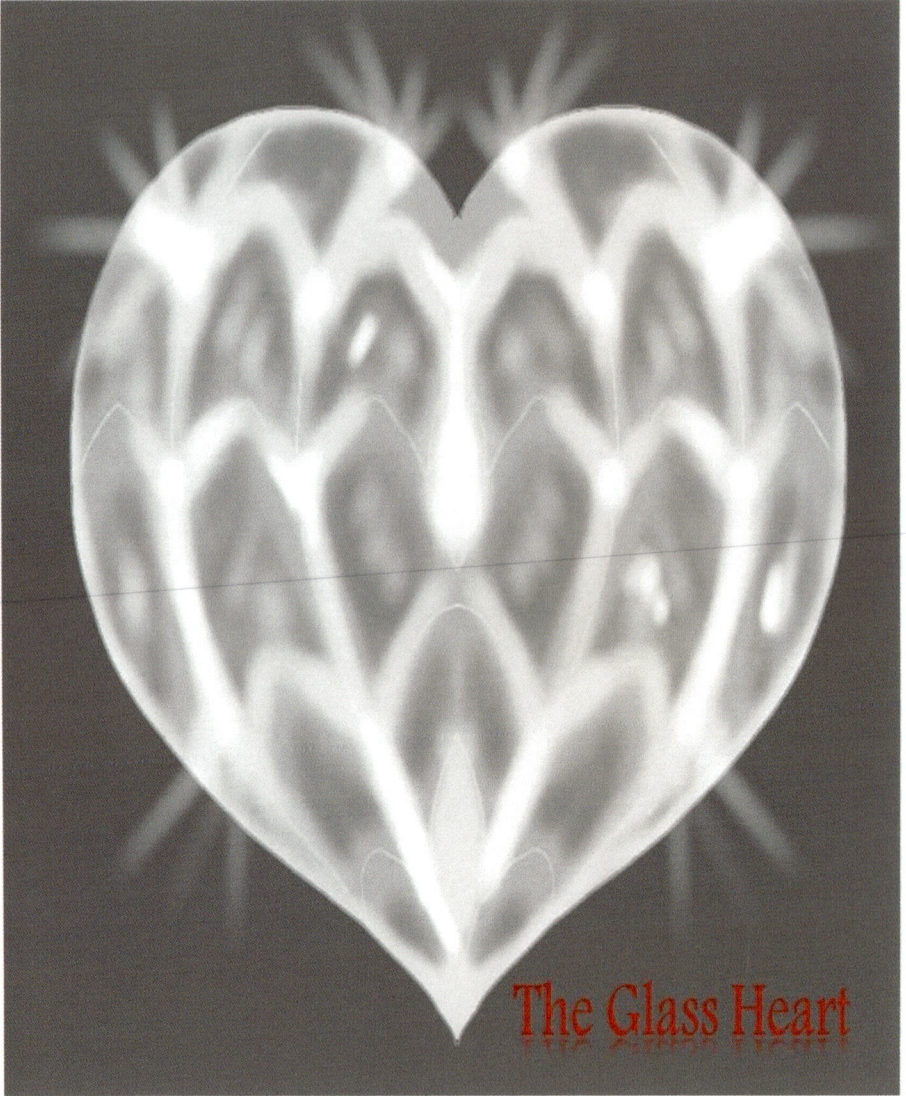
The Glass Heart

The Glass Heart

How we live….

Beautiful, reflective, and helpful, the Glass Heart is able to allow light to shine through them effortlessly. Those with a Glass Heart respond well to everything in moderation, as extreme cold or extreme heat will tend to splinter, fracture, or weaken them. Most Glass Hearts are very accomplished, or experts in their field, but you might not ever know it.

How we love…..

Once splintered the Glass Heart has the ability to shatter with each successive stress. Protecting themselves from injury will make the Glass Heart seem distant, when in reality they are simply deciding whether they can trust you with their heart.

That is not to say that the Glass Heart is afraid of life; rather the opposite. Generous with their time and talents, they are more than willing to risk all for a good cause or those they love deeply. They are very aware of their ability to cut deeply when threatened, and often, when people misjudge them, they can withdraw from others for a period of time, often emerging with new insight.

How we learn….

Naturally waterproof, Glass Hearts work best within smaller groups or one-on-one types of occupations because they are able to let most thoughtless comments roll easily off their backs. They keep their knowledge and credentials concealed until the right moment. Great listeners, they analyze the situation before committing and are very strategic. Glass Hearts are eager to learn new things but approach the process with careful consideration and mindfulness.

The Glass Heart is able to allow light to shine through them effortlessly.

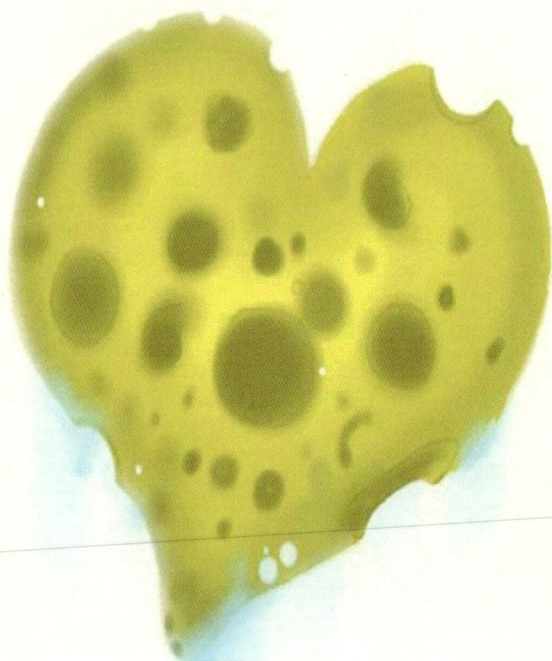

The Sponge Heart

The Sponge Heart

How we live....

Compassionate, caring, and kind, the Sponge Heart has great depths of sympathy and empathy that allow them to reach out to others. Those with a Sponge Heart often find themselves working with those who have experienced great hardship and trouble, due in large part to the fact that the sponge heart has a great capacity to 'be there' for others.

Not only does the Sponge take on the world's problems but they believe they can solve the world's problems. Because of this, the sponge has great ideas and loves to share them. Spiritual and trustworthy, many Sponge Hearts may work in service-oriented professions, working as ministers, counselors, and non-profit organizations.

How we love.....

Sponge Hearts have a great capacity to take on volumes of love. They tend to absorb others' problems, filling up their 'sponge' heart until it is so full that they often experience burnout and a sense of overwhelm.

The good news is that the Sponge Heart can be wrung out and bounce back into their original shape. The Sponge Heart is one of the most forgiving and resilient hearts. Detail oriented, Sponge Hearts never forget a birthday, anniversary, or holiday and are extremely involved with their families.

How we learn....

Sponge Hearts make the day to day world function and thrive on involvement with others. Truly caring and sympathetic, Sponge Hearts must learn to first love themselves as much as they care for those around them. This allows the sponge heart to remain balanced with not too much water, nor too little. The Sponge Heart soaks up knowledge, often becoming an expert in their field. People seek out the Sponge Heart for advice and they are always happy to oblige.

Sponge Hearts are a blessing to others.

The Kaleidoscope Heart

The Kaleidoscope Heart

How we live....

Reflective, insightful, energetic, and innovative, the Kaleidoscope Heart lives a dynamic life that for many would appear hectic...but to the Kaleidoscope Heart, it is in harmonic balance. The word, Kaleidoscope, comes from several Greek words meaning 'beautiful form' and this holds true for the Kaleidoscope Heart. Always seeking things to share with the world, reflecting, and seeking the truth, this heart type will always see the real person inside. They love to share life experiences through art, photography, and storytelling.

Discerning, intelligent, and often driven, the Kaleidoscope Heart has the ability to make something wonderful out of those things that are most often overlooked or discarded.

How we love.....

Kaleidoscope Hearts may be peacemakers, healers, and someone who can reach the 'unreachable'. Like their namesakes, they diffuse incoming light, so that the beauty of the small pieces of glass or beads held within can be seen and appreciated. Kaleidoscope Hearts love to hold others up, encouraging them to shine. They love nature and adventure, often seeking relationships with others who share the same interests.

How we learn....

Kaleidoscope Hearts are very precise by nature and love to have things ordered in a way that makes sense to them (even if it seems chaotic to others). Trusting the Kaleidoscope Heart to always have the best interest of others in mind allows them to shine, and rise to any challenge. Kaleidoscope Hearts love to learn new activities, skills, and can achieve anything they put their mind to. Each day is a new day and a new design of their own making.

Kaleidoscope Hearts reflect the light that shines around them.

The Fire Heart

The Fire Heart

Passionate, energetic, and warm, the Fire Heart is blessed with the innate ability to inspire, soothe, and heal. Many Fire Hearted people find themselves in the healing arts, or in the creative fields of endeavor; anywhere their flame can grow and glow the hottest and the brightest.

Eager and bright, the Fire Heart loves to take in as much 'fuel' as it can, either from the physical or the spiritual.

How we love…..

Fire Hearts are often great pranksters and love to smolder quietly until they roar into life, often becoming the center of attention. When the Fire Heart flames out of control, without regard for others, relationships can become scalded and singed. However, A Fire Heart can be injured when others around them seek to control them, misuse them, or otherwise attempt to keep them hidden. Excessive sorrow, like a rainstorm, will often be too much for the Fire Heart and cause the light to go out.

How we learn….

Fire Hearts are the innovators and the visionaries that fuel progress and success. Enjoying well deserved accolades and praise make the Fire Heart want to do even more. Truly energetic and willing to take on any task, the Fire Heart must learn to trust others as well as they trust themselves.

Whether glowing brightly or slowly simmering, the Fire Heart never misses an opportunity to warm others.

25

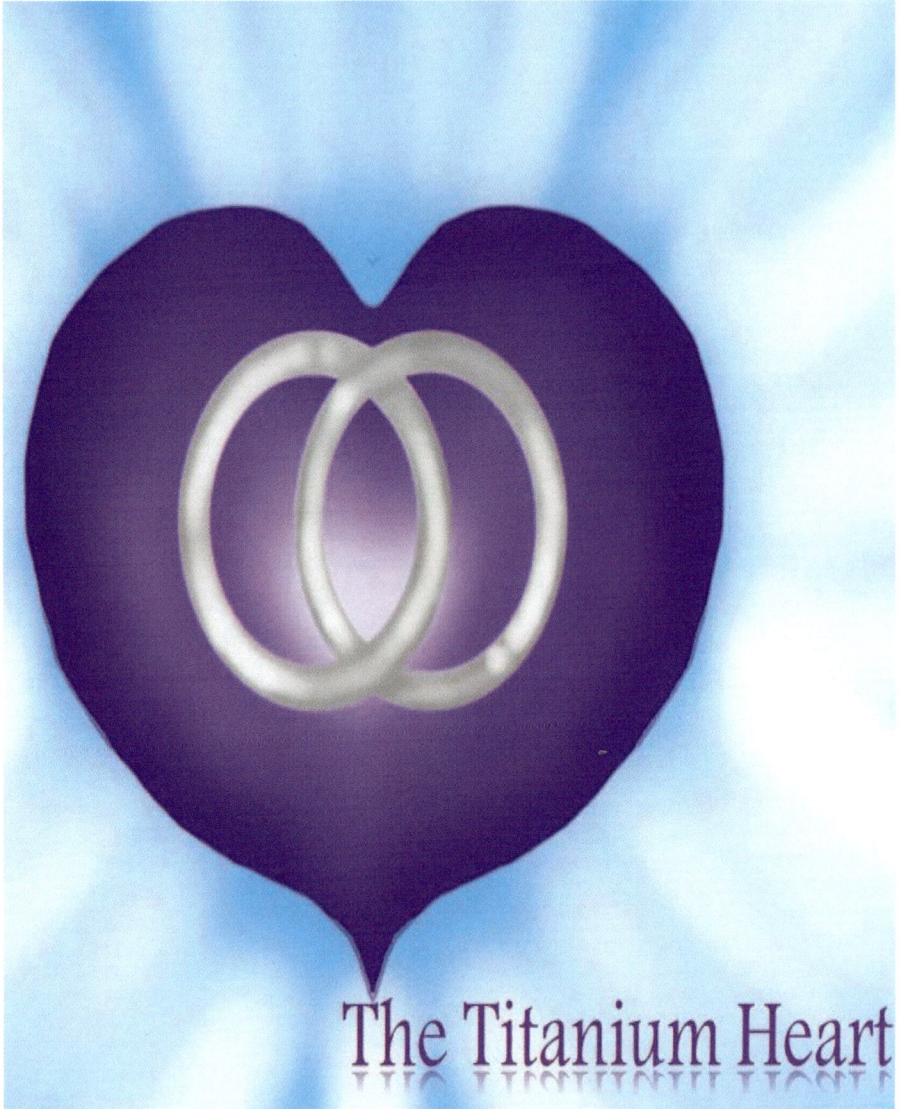

The Titanium Heart

The Titanium Heart

The calm in the storm, the wisdom in spite of pain, the one person who is able to find the silver lining, the Titanium Heart lives selflessly and is devoted to doing good deeds for mankind. They are humble and live for a greater reward, and as a result possess a deep understanding of life. Their prayers are powerful.

How we love…..

Titanium Hearts love God and family. They have a different perspective on life, which gives them a unique insight into relationships. Titanium Hearts are durable and once committed they will never forsake you. Two rings forged together can resist anything life throws their way. Kind and considerate, they focus on all things good and they see the beauty in all people. The actions or words of mankind cannot dent them or corrode their spirit. Titanium Hearts fear God, not man, and they speak the truth in love.

How we learn….

Titanium Hearts seek wisdom and spiritual enlightenment, and are constantly searching for the meaning of life. They will travel to distant lands to gain knowledge about different cultures and religions, and have a need to witness to the lost and accept all people. They love to connect with other enlightened people and might pursue degrees in Theology or Religious Studies. From an early age, Titanium Hearts are keenly aware that they were created to do great things and that God is guiding their life.

They understand what God has to offer and they live what they learn.

For More information on The Heart Guide, products, or to contact the author, please visit The Heart Guide on Twitter,

Facebook, or contact:

Sgthornton1@gmail.com

37167921R00019

Made in the USA
Charleston, SC
27 December 2014